North-East England

LANDSCAPES

Graeme Peacock

MYRIAD

LONDON

First published in 2006
by Myriad Books Limited,
35 Bishopsthorpe Road,
London SE26 4PA

ISBN 1 904 736 15 7

Designed by Jerry Goldie
Graphic Design
Printed in China

www.myriadbooks.com

Photographs on pages 3, 109, 114,
115, 116, 117, 118, 119, 120, 121, 123, 124,
125, 126, 128 by Mike Kipling
Photography
www.mikekipling.com

Title page: celebrations during
the Tall Ships Race, Newcastle;
right: looking along Hadrian's
Wall from Housesteads;
far right: the Transporter Bridge,
Middlesbrough

Contents

Northumberland

The county of Northumberland is a world that is waiting to be explored – a rich mix of splendid rolling landscapes, pretty market towns, characterful coastal villages, magnificent castles and beautiful country houses. It is an area in which pivotal developments in the history of the British Isles have unfolded – from the construction of Hadrian's Wall, which marked the northern outpost of the Roman empire, to the arrival of St Aidan on Holy Island (below), bringing Christianity to England. Centuries after the Romans had left, the county was still a battleground – Dunstanburgh Castle (right) was used to supply men and horses for Edward II's invasion of Scotland and bloody conflicts either side of the Border were to continue for hundreds of years. Today, this history is there to be discovered, among the "far horizons" of the county's unique landscape.

Berwick

Trapped inside the Elizabethan walls of 1596 that enclose the town, much of Berwick-upon-Tweed's ancient street pattern still survives. Parts of Edward I's castle can still be seen, with its famous White Wall descending down the hill towards the river like some medieval staircase. In this violent period the town changed hands between England and Scotland 13 times before finally surrendering to the English in 1482.

The old harbour that played such an important part in the history of Berwick is still

to be seen with the wealthy merchants' houses and doorways to their cellars cut through the walls. Just upstream, with its arches reflected in the water, is the long narrow Old Bridge; its 15 arches were built between 1611 and 1624. The bridge carried the Great North Road until 1928 when the Royal Tweed Bridge with its four massive spans of reinforced concrete was built to improve the flow of traffic.

In the surrounding countryside small villages such as Etal, with its thatched pub and houses with unusually large roof slates, still fascinate the visitor.

Lindisfarne Castle, Holy Island

The posts that stand in front of Lindisfarne Castle on Holy Island are the remains of a jetty where lime was loaded onto ships bound for Dundee in the 1870s. Further evidence of this trade can be found in the huge limekilns still standing beneath the castle.

Built around the year 1550 from stones robbed from the nearby priory, the castle was designed to offer protection to the harbour, which had become a strategic naval base guarding against possible raids by the Scots. It saw action during the Civil War and was briefly captured by two supporters of the Scottish cause in 1715. Even though it continued to be garrisoned it gradually declined and was last used by an artillery detachment in the 1860s after which it began to fall into disrepair.

In 1902 the castle was bought by Edward Hudson, the founder of *Country Life* magazine. He employed Sir Edwin Lutyens to restore the building and convert it into a home. In 1944 the castle was given to the National Trust.

Christianity and Holy Island

To stand in front of St Aidan's statue and look out toward Lindisfarne Castle is to experience the history of Holy Island. St Aidan's torch brings the light of the Gospels to the world whereas the castle is a reminder of the island's military past. The priory we can see today was founded in 1132 as a daughter house of the Benedictine Abbey of Durham. The threat of invasion and war was still great so the monks felt it was necessary to include the battlements which can still clearly be seen on the outer wall.

St Aidan founded a far older monastery here in 635. This older monastery was sacked by the Vikings in 793, the first such raid on a monastery in England. Before this time civilisation flowered here and the Lindisfarne Gospels were produced. The island will be forever associated with St Aidan and today his bronze statue can be seen in the grounds of the priory.

Cuthbert's Isle

To the west of Holy Island is the small rocky outcrop known as Cuthbert's Isle. St Cuthbert had a small hermitage and chapel here around 670; a short walk across the rock pools at low tide will bring you to the site of the chapel marked by a large cross. The island also offers superb views of the mudflats and surrounding countryside.

Some 500 years later St Cuthbert's successors built the magnificent arch of the west doorway to the priory that clearly bears the hallmarks of its Norman builders. Behind it, but clearly visible, is the "rainbow arch", originally one of the ribs that supported the huge vault of the church which has somehow miraculously survived down the centuries. This section of the priory was the monks' church and the columns still have their original chevrons clearly visible upon them. Today the priory and castle are in the care of English Heritage and this is one of its most popular sites.

Lindisfarne sunrise

A midsummer sunrise behind Lindisfarne Castle paints the mudflats exposed at low tide with a vibrant palette of reds and yellows. Still a working harbour, fishermen leave here every day while mussels are harvested from beds just off the shore. Two hundred yards to the north of the castle is the small walled garden designed by Gertude Jeykll in 1903. This enchanting garden is now maintained, along with the castle, by the National Trust.

To the east of the castle are three upturned boats, now used as storage. Close to the castle are the huge 19th-century limekilns. The lime was quarried on the north of the island and brought down on a wagon way that is still used as a footpath.

Large parts of the island and surrounding tidal flats are a nature reserve. The island attracts a great many birdwatchers, particularly in autumn and winter when migratory birds are plentiful.

11

Holy Island Church

On its southern wall Holy Island's parish church of St Mary the Virgin shows the erosion where the wind has picked out the weakness of the stones. To the east of the church is the stump of the old village cross, called the "petting stone", over which brides assisted by two fishermen jump to ensure a happy marriage.

An earlier wooden church dating from around 700 stood here; the link with St Cuthbert is reinforced by the beautiful chancel carpet woven in the design of St Mark's Gospel from the Lindisfarne Gospels created by the monks on the island. There is also a wooden sculpture showing the monks carrying St Cuthbert's body on their journey to Durham. Above the chancel arch some original Saxon work can still be seen.

Three arches on the northern arcade date from the 12th century and it is believed that they are the only examples in Northumberland of arches showing the alternate use of red and white stones.

Bamburgh Castle

Perched on its huge rock Bamburgh Castle can be seen for miles around; it dominates the pretty village below, clustered around its wooded green. The churchyard has a monument to Grace Darling together with the graves of victims of shipwrecks on the nearby Farne Islands.

The first known fortification here was a wooden palisade built around 547, although the site had been occupied since the Iron Age. The castle's name comes from that of Bebba, the wife of Ethelfrith who ruled Northumbria from 593 to 616, and it soon became known as Bebbanburgh. Its huge Norman keep has walls some 11ft (3m) thick; the building we see today is a combination of restoration by Lord Crewe, Bishop of Durham in the 18th century and then later by the first Lord Armstrong, the Victorian industrialist.

Standing on the shoreline and looking up to the castle it is easy to see why it is such a favourite with film directors. Its iconic status and the golden sands of the beaches below combine to make Bamburgh a magnet for visitors.

The Farne Islands

It was from the Longstone lighthouse that Grace Darling and her father rowed out to rescue the survivors of the shipwrecked *Forfarshire*. Flashing once every 20 seconds night and day the light was built between 1825 and 1826; it became fully automatic in 1980.

The Farne Islands are owned by the National Trust and consist of a group of islands 2.5 miles (4km) off the fishing village of Seahouses; of these, islands 15 and 28 are visible depending on the state of the tide, and they form one of Britain's most important seabird sanctuaries. The closest island is Inner Farne and the furthest out, at 4.4 miles (7km) from the shore, is Knivestone. The chapel on Inner Farne is built on the site of St Cuthbert's Oratory and was restored in the 19th century. Lit by a beautiful stained-glass window the serene interior is decorated with oak panelling, screens and stalls brought from Durham Cathedral. The font in the foreground is a favourite nesting place for Arctic terns.

Often referred to as "Europe's Galapagos", the Farnes have over 50,000 pairs of nesting puffins and an additional 48,000 pairs of other species.

Beadnell

The sun sets over the cobles nestling in the harbour of Beadnell. This fishing port is very unusual: despite the fact that it is on the east coast, the harbour was built so it can only be entered by boats approaching from the west. In the late 1700s the huge sweep of Beadnell Bay was popular for horse-racing and at the time the village was well known as a centre for smuggling.

The beach at Beadnell is capped at its northern end by the harbour and limekilns. Dating from 1789 these huge kilns were last used for lime production in the 1820s; later they were used for herring curing. In the summer up to 60 local fishermen worked the keel boats operating out of the harbour often accompanied by boats from Cornwall and Scotland. Today, Beadnell is not only a working fishing village but also one of the most popular holiday beaches in the region.

Fierce storms breached the harbour wall in 1997 leaving a massive hole. Just outside, on the main road, among the trees, is one of Britain's last surviving AA telephone boxes.

Druridge Bay

The sweeping sands and grassy dunes of Druridge Bay are seen above, in a view which looks north to Amble Harbour. The beach provides a focal point for the country park sited on land restored from the Coldrife open cast coalmine which was active until the 1960s.

Seahouses

Tourist boats and fishing vessels sit side by side in Seahouses harbour. Seahouses grew out of the village of North Sunderland when the fishermen built the "sea houses" by the side of the harbour. For a while the village was known by the name of North Sunderland Sea-Houses.

The flat roof behind the old limekilns betrays the fact that a railway bringing the raw materials once terminated on top of it. The lime industry flourished up until the 1850s when the fishing industry took over, fuelled by the demand for herring – the demand was so great that in 1834 over 6,000 barrels of salted herring were dispatched to the Baltic States and Germany. As a result, a new harbour was built at a cost of £25,000, opening in June 1889.

Dunstanburgh

Today the west curtain wall of Dunstanburgh Castle is somewhat fragmented. The most notable feature along its length is the Lilburn Tower, which is clearly visible for miles around. Dating from 1323 its ground floor would have held provisions while the upper floor provided accommodation for the garrison. Dunstanburgh's strategic importance can easily be seen from the vantage point of her towers. Looking south towards the small village of Craster the coast sweeps southwards towards Newton and Howick eventually arriving at Alnmouth, Amble and Coquet Island.

In the early 1380s major alterations to the castle were carried out by John of Gaunt. Among these are the stark remains of the great gatehouse that, unusually, doubled as a keep; this still conveys the power of this wonderful building. It would have been necessary for any attacking force trying to gain access to the castle to go through this narrow passage and they would be exposed to fire from above and below. The castle was given to the Ministry of Works in 1929 and today it is in the care of English Heritage.

Alnmouth cross

This cross on the southern side of the Aln estuary marks the site of the original village church of Alnmouth. In 1806 a great storm blew up which forced the Aln to change course and cut the church off from the village. In 1207 the village was granted a charter for a port and a market. In the 18th century the main export was grain and many of the granaries can still be seen, now converted into houses. Imports into Alnwick included slates, timber and guano. Once derided by the preacher John Wesley as a wicked place, today Alnmouth is a sleepy little village at the mouth of the river Aln.

Alnwick marketplace

The marketplace in Alnwick has long been a meeting place for the people of the town and dates back to the 1200s. With its cafes, shops, cobbled surface and market cross the area forms the ideal location for the town's music festivals and craft and farmer's markets. The buildings that surround the square are varied in their age and architecture; the town hall, built in 1771, is not owned by the council but by the "freemen of Alnwick".

Standing some 83ft (25m) high the fine fluted stone Tenantry Column has an internal staircase leading to a gallery at the top. It was raised in 1816 by grateful tenants of the Duke of Northumberland, who reduced their rents after the Napoleonic wars to alleviate their hardship. The Duke then decided that if they could afford such a gesture they could afford the rents and he promptly raised them again. Thus the column is known locally as the "Farmer's Folly".

Alnwick Castle

Often called the Windsor of the North, the rolling fields and scattered copses betray the hand of the famous landscape gardener Capability Brown who laid out Alnwick's grounds in the 18th century. The 14th-century barbican at Alnwick is one of the most impressive in the country. Built as a motte and bailey castle by the Normans it was acquired by the de Vescys in 1090 and in 1309 passed into the hands of the Percys.

The castle was restored in the 19th century and today the walls look over the river Aln and the landscaped park below. Every Shrove Tuesday the two parishes of the town play each other here in a unique game of football, a tradition that goes back centuries. The lion of the Percy family stares at all who drive into the town from the north and thus gives the bridge its name. It figures prominently in Turner's painting of the castle by moonlight and offers superb views of the parkland. Although open to the public the castle remains the private family home of the Dukes of Northumberland.

Alnwick Castle

The centre of Alnwick Castle consists of a large, fortified block set around a small courtyard and containing the most important rooms. The imposing walls which surround the castle are dotted with large towers at various intervals and these are used today to house special exhibitions. About one sixth of the outer wall has been reduced to ground level over the centuries to open up views into the park. The castle is often used as a location for films and television; two block-busting movies – *Harry Potter and the Philosopher's Stone* and *Harry Potter and the Chamber of Secrets* were filmed here. The castle also appeared in the first series of the television comedy *Blackadder*.

Alnwick Garden and Treehouse

Enclosed by walls which are 250 years old, Alnwick Garden is believed to be one of the largest walled gardens in the world. On entering the visitor is greeted by the Grand Cascade where 7,260 gallons of water per minute tumble down 27 weirs, disappearing into four large bell mouth openings, to reappear at the other side of a walkway in four "mounds" of water. The three large central jets reach a height of 20ft (6m), with 40 smaller jets sending water 15ft (5m) into the air. These are complemented by 80 side jets that create sweeping curves of water to the centre of the Cascade.

Outside the walls of the main garden is one of the

world's largest wooden treehouses, an enormous structure of turret-topped buildings and amazing walkways in the sky that link the different sections.

The site on which Alnwick garden is built has had a colourful history, with gardens being planted here by leading contemporary designers.

25

Amble Harbour at sunset

The sun sinks slowly over the marina at Amble which is host to around 250 boats and yachts. In the days when Amble was a thriving port the sailors from the various countries who traded here called it "the friendliest port" due to the hospitality they received.

Officially known as Warkworth harbour, Amble harbour was constructed in 1839 and owes its existence to its coal exports. Although one of Northumberland's most important fishing ports, Amble today also has an excellent yacht marina and is renowned for leisure sailing. Compared to other ports Amble still has a large fishing fleet and is regarded as a traditional working port. Boatbuilding has always been carried on in the town and it continues to this day. The larger fishing boats that moor along the harbour wall land a variety of fish, crabs, lobsters and prawns and working cobles can still be seen in the inner harbour.

Chillingham

The large cannons that sit outside Chillingham Castle bear witness to the violent past of one of Northumberland's most fascinating castles. Now a stately home open to the public, Chillingham Castle has seen more than its fair share of border warfare and is reputed to be one of the most haunted houses in the county. Amongst the ghosts is Lady Mary Berkeley whose rustling dress can still be heard along the corridors and stairs accompanied by a chilling blast of air.

The present structure dates from 1344 when Sir Thomas Grey built a courtyard and curtain wall around an old pele tower. In 1590 the main entrance was moved to its present position, in preparation for the visit of King James VI of Scotland on his journey south to London for his coronation.

Blyth Beach

To the north and south of Blyth's harbour entrance are wide open beaches. Much of the coastline to the north consists of sand dunes with their typical grasses and habitats. Like other ports in Northumberland, Blyth owes its present size to the development of the coal industry, reaching its peak in the 1960s. Nowadays large wind vanes can be seen on the harbour wall supplying electricity. This row of nine 300kw Windmaster turbines generates green electricity. At the time, the turbines were the largest erected offshore in the world.

In the middle ages the beaches either side of the estuary were sited next to saltpans which provided the town with a thriving trade. Today Blyth is a bustling, modern port. The town is also well-known for its "Lighthouse in the street". It was built in 1788 by Sir Matthew White Ridley who owned Cowpen Colliery and had his own wharf at the harbour. Then, the lighthouse stood only 10 yards from the sea wall but continuous development over the years has resulted in it now being positioned in a back lane.

Belsay Hall and Castle

Sir Charles Monck was greatly influenced by the art and culture of the ancient Greeks. In 1817 he decided to build a Grecian-style house on his estate at Belsay and employed some of the finest craftsmen of the day to do so.

Belsay Hall has one of the most beautiful and fascinating gardens in Northumberland. It is full of corridors, arches and ravines with vines, ferns, palms and exotic and rare plants. In the late 19th and early 20th centuries Sir Charles' grandson Sir Arthur Middleton extended the garden and introduced rhododendrons and other plants new to the country at the time.

In the grounds of the estate is the original Belsay Castle, a conglomeration of building styles completed down through the ages. The original castle was a tower house built around 1360 which still has its battlements and arrow vents. In the early 17th century a two-storied range was built alongside and in 1717 a further wing was added although little remains of this extension today.

Morpeth

The river Wansbeck flows sedately through Morpeth, one of the major market towns of Northumberland. The footbridge shown here is actually built on the abutments and central piers of the medieval bridge that crossed the river and was destroyed in 1832. By the side of the main bridge, built by Thomas Telford in 1831, is a block of buildings that are relics of the 13th-century chantry chapel of All Saints where tolls were collected and which was also a school. The school was attended by William Turner (1508-1568), the "Father of English Botany". Little remains of the castle as it was burnt by King John and virtually destroyed in the Civil War. Emily Davison, the suffragette killed by the king's horse in the 1913 Derby, is buried near to the castle. Admiral Collingwood, Nelson's second-in-command at Trafalgar, hailed from Morpeth; his home can be seen in Oldgate Street.

Cambo

Set back from the main road, Cambo has an air of tranquillity. The village consists of a group of terraced cottages enclosing a square with a walled green and several well-stocked, attractive private walled gardens.

Cambo was first laid out as a model village in 1740. An early chapel dating from the 12th to the 15th centuries was demolished in 1875, but a few coffin lids were preserved and are now set into the walls of the present church which was consecrated in 1842 and built by Sir John Trevelyan. He owned Wallington Hall (below) and several members of the Trevelyan family are buried in the churchyard. The old schoolhouse (left) which was altered and enlarged in 1911, had as one of its younger pupils Capability Brown.

Wallington Hall

Unlike other great houses in Northumberland, Wallington is sited close to a main road on the other side of which is the walled garden. The four magnificent stone griffin heads which sit at the roadside are said to have adorned one of London's original mediaeval gateways.

A castle which was once owned by the famous Fenwick family of Northumberland once stood here and the present house is sited on its cellars. A square house was built on top of a Tudor mansion when Sir John Fenwick sold it to Sir William Blackett in 1688. Work began on the present house in 1783 by Sir Walter Calverly Blackett. In 1846 Sir Walter Trevelyan inherited it; the extensive gardens were landscaped by local man Lancelot "Capability Brown", the famous landscape gardener who was born at nearby Kirkharle.

Hadrian's Wall

One can imagine how a Roman soldier who hailed from the warm climates of Spain or Greece must have longed for the sun of his homeland during the cold Northumberland winters. Today the wall and its environs can be equally bleak even for the modern visitor.

The magnificent beauty of the winter landscape around Hadrian's Wall is seen here in this view looking towards Housesteads; it shows how the Romans made use of the steep slopes of the Whin Sill as a major defensive element in the construction and siting of the wall.

Forts and watchtowers

The Romans designed the wall to be part of an overall defensive system consisting of forts and watchtowers. In this region of Northumberland the Roman fort of Vindolanda was used to accommodate the local Roman soldiers. Amongst the many tablets found on the site are requests for warm woollen clothing to be sent to the legionaries from home. These notes are remarkably similar to the letters sent home from soldiers in the trenches in the First World War.

Housesteads

Built when the Roman Empire was at its height, Housesteads is the best-preserved example of a Roman fort in the country. It held a garrison of around a thousand men, most of whom were German auxiliaries. Unlike other forts along the wall, Housesteads is built on quite a noticeable slope; the Romans sited their granaries on the highest part of the fort to keep the food inside dry. During the time of the reivers (cross-border raiders who were both Scots and English) Housesteads became a hiding place for raiders, cattle rustlers and their booty.

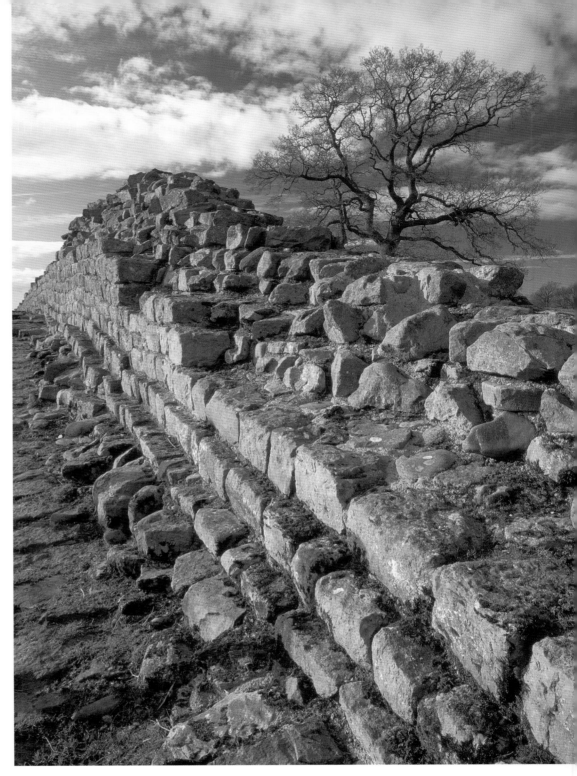

Birdoswald

Birdoswald has one of the most spectacular locations of any fort on the Roman wall as it stands on a high spur of land overlooking the Irthing Gorge. You can still see parts of the original turf wall built in AD122. A small museum illustrates the lives of the soldiers who were stationed on this unfriendly outpost of empire.

The stone from Hadrian's Wall was looted over the centuries and used for other buildings in nearby towns and farms, resulting in the piecemeal structure we can see today. The Romans also reduced the width of the wall, using fewer stones as they progressed west. Sycamore Gap (far left, above) is one of the best-known places on the wall. It shows how the Romans, when building it, followed the lie of the land exactly.

Corbridge

The countryside around Corbridge is particularly noted for its beauty and the town's parks and riverside walks are very popular. The Northumberland Show is held annually in the fields outside the town and draws visitors and exhibitors from all over the county.

One of the most important supply depots for Hadrian's Wall was at Corbridge just north of the present town. It occupied a strategic position at the point where the Stanegate, the road running parallel with the wall towards Carlisle, met Dere Street, the main road into Scotland where it crossed the Tyne. Much of the stone from the site was used to build Hexham Abbey and parts of Corbridge itself.

The bridge at Corbridge was built in 1674 and still gives access to one of Northumberland's most interesting towns. It was so well built that it was the only bridge on the Tyne to withstand the great flood of 1771 when it was said the water was so high that people could lean over the parapet and wash their hands. Corbridge is known for its quaint town centre and individual shops and is an ideal base for exploring the beauty of Northumberland.

Prudhoe and Langley castles

The name Prudhoe means "proud hill". The castle, which lies on the south bank of the Tyne, is protected on the east by a steep ravine and is partly enclosed by a deep moat. It is first mentioned in 1173 when it was besieged by the Scots shortly after it was built by Odinel d'Umfreville.

William the Lion of Scotland besieged the castle again one year later. The castle remained a fortress of the Umfrevilles until 1381 when it passed to the Percys. By the 19th century the castle had fallen into disuse and is now in the care of English Heritage.

Langley Castle, below, looks much as it did when it was first built in 1364. It was the stronghold of the Lucy family but after only 50 years it was gutted by fire, perhaps on the orders of Henry IV. Since that time however the castle has been a fortress, a private house, a barracks during the Second World War and a girls' public school until it finally became the hotel it is today.

Linhope Spout

This dramatic 50ft (15m) high waterfall is in the Breamish Valley a few miles to the west of Powburn. It lies on the Linhope Burn, a tributary of the river Breamish. The best time to visit is in midsummer, preferably after a long spell of rain.

Kielder Water

The largest artificial lake in Europe, Kielder Water holds a staggering 200 billion litres of water which supplies the people and the industries of the north-east. Kielder Castle was built in 1775 as a shooting lodge for the Duke of Northumberland and now acts as the main visitor centre for the park, which has become a centre for recreational activities such as sailing, canoeing, cycling and birdwatching. Fontburn Reservoir (left) is a similarly popular and picturesque fishery. It nestles in an idyllic setting south of the Simonside Hills near Rothbury.

Rothbury

Rothbury, with its sloping green shaded by sycamores, is known as the capital of Coquetdale and serves a vast area of rural Northumberland. Its shops and facilities bordering the long tree-lined green and the open countryside around make it a popular destination for visitors and locals alike. The Anglo-Saxons had a royal burgh here and the town was an ancient barony passing through various owners before coming into the hands of the Percy family in the 1330s. Rectors from the village church can be traced back to 1107 and in 1291 King Edward I granted a charter for a market here every Thursday and a fair annually. The name "Rothbury" is possibly derived from the Celtic word *rhath* meaning a cleared spot, or from the Saxon warrior called Hrotha whose kingdom was in this area. Its first recorded name is "Rodeberia".

The Simonside Hills lie within the Northumberland National Park and are formed from a dramatic sandstone escarpment. They offer easy walking with fine views especially in the northern sector overlooking Rothbury where the famous Lordenshaws hill fort can be found.

Yeavering Bell Hill Fort

The largest Iron Age hill fort in the region, Yeavering Bell lies on the edge of the Cheviot Hills some three miles north of Wooler, enclosing some 13 acres (5.2ha). Its most remarkable feature is a massive stone-walled rampart, in places some 12ft (4m) wide, which encloses much of the summit and can be easily seen from the roads below.

Inside the fort are traces of 130 hut platforms. Beyond the main wall which encloses all of the summit are additional defensive stone outworks on the east and west sides. An entire town existed here some 2,000 years ago until it was abandoned sometime around the 1st century. It is not clear why but the walls do appear to have been deliberately flattened which suggests that the Romans may have destroyed the fort.

After the Roman withdrawal, the fort was reoccupied for a time remaining in use and being rebuilt at least four or five times, up until the reign of King Edwin in the 7th century.

Elsdon

The Vicar's pele tower at Elsdon was built about 1400 and has walls 9ft (3m) thick. The village also has the spectacular remains of a Norman motte and bailey castle and is noted for its large sloping green and the nearby Winter's Gibbet. One of the rectors here was the Reverend Charles Dodgson who, from 1762 to 1765, was a tutor to the Duke of Northumberland's son. He was also the great grandfather of Lewis Carroll, the author of *Alice in Wonderland*.

The village is noted for its massive motte and bailey castle built by Robert d'Umfraville in the 11th century. The Battle of Otterburn was fought close by and some of the dead were buried under Elsdon Church which stands on the broad village green.

Coquetdale

A misty dawn rises over the beautiful Coquetdale valley announcing its presence by bathing the rocks and heather in an orange light. Coquetdale has a timeless air about it; with its bracken and rocky outcrops it is easy to imagine the valley's earliest human inhabitants carving the many cup and ring mark patterns, and horsemen driving stolen cattle along the river's edge.

Harbottle dominates the valley and is home to the castle where Margaret, Countess of Lennox, grandmother of James VI of Scotland and I of England, was born. The valley offers stunning scenery all year round and is part of the Northumberland National Park.

A few miles up the valley, where the Coquet meets the Alwin, is Alwinton, now famous for its Border Shepherds show, the last of the many agricultural shows that are held throughout the region. Heading north out of the village is Clennel Street, one of the great droving roads that heads northwards to the border.

Cragside (right)

With its mixture of German, French and Old English styles Cragside has a majestic appearance and is surrounded by a 1000-acre (404ha) forest garden. In fact with its hot and cold running water, fire alarms, central heating, telephones and a Turkish bath it was known as "The Palace of the Magician".

Home to William Armstrong, the north-east's leading industrialist of his day, the house was begun in 1869 and finished in 1884. It was the first house in the world to be lit and powered by hydroelectricity. Lakes were created to make stunning vistas and azaleas and rhododendrons planted to give the astounding displays for which the estate is famous. Over 7m trees and bushes were planted and hundreds of boulders were manhandled into position to create a fantastic rock garden with tumbling waterfalls and scenic views from bridges and paths.

Shillmoor

Shillmoor in the upper Coquet valley is typical of the type of farm and small settlement to be found in this area. Rising above the farm is Shillhope Law, a particularly popular summit with walkers which gives fine views of the Cheviots. Much of the surrounding area is used for military training and it is not unusual to see troops on exercise.

Tyne and Wear

Newcastle upon Tyne, Gateshead and Sunderland have a rich history based on a legacy of famous industries and civic tradition. In the last decade the area has re-emerged from a period of decline with innovative architecture and high-tech industries. The renovation of historic town and city centres has made the area one of the most dynamic in the UK. Massive investment in urban design and public art, including Antony Gormley's sculpture the Angel of the North (below) and splendid new additions to the Quayside including the Millennium Bridge (right) have transformed the image of the north-east. But the region has not neglected its heritage. Its Roman past has been preserved and celebrated at such visitor attractions as Arbeia Roman fort and Segedunum; historic towns like North Shields and Cullercoats have beeen restored and, in Sunderland, the Winter Gardens and the Empire have been gloriously re-built and refurbished for the 21st century.

Seaton Sluice

Dawn breaks over the harbour of Seaton Sluice. In the 17th century the mouth of Seaton Burn was treacherous and awkward for craft wanting to use the port. To alleviate the problem, in 1660 Sir Ralph Delaval built a stone pier to create a harbour. In 1690 Sir Ralph added sluice gates which closed as the incoming tide filled the harbour. At low tide the sluice gates were opened and a powerful flood of water flushed the harbour clean thus giving the port its name of Seaton Sluice.

By 1764 a great cut was made into the cliff enabling the water of the harbour to take a short route to the sea instead of travelling around in a curve. A major engineering feat in its day the "cut", or "gut" as it is now called locally, was some 886ft (270m long), 30ft (9m) wide and 49ft (15m) deep. At one point the harbour rivalled North Shields as it gave employment to hundreds of sailors and provided a living for miners, shipbuilders and rope and sailmakers.

Seaton Sluice Sands

To the north of the harbour of Seaton Sluice is an area of dunes and a long sandy beach. The sand dunes cover an area called Hartley Links which forms a protective barrier between the sea and the land. There have been attempts to protect this fragile environment by planting marram grass to help bind the dunes and stabilise them. This is a wonderful area in which to walk and enjoy views of the harbour and beach.

Seaton Sluice port

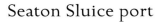

Lying at the very southern border of the Northumberland coastline at the mouth of Seaton Burn, Seaton Sluice is made up of two separate villages, Seaton Sluice and Old Hartley; over the years they have gradually merged into one village. Looking at Seaton Sluice today with its small fishing boats and leisure craft it is difficult to imagine it as a busy commercial port. In the 18th century as well as locally produced salt, the harbour also exported coal and bottles. In 1763 Sir Francis Delaval established the Royal Hartley Bottleworks and the buildings dominated the harbour. It soon became the largest bottle making factory in England and helped establish the skills of glass and bottlemaking in the north-east.

St Mary's Lighthouse

Lit up at night, St Mary's Lighthouse not only makes a beautiful reflection in the rock pools at low tide but also reveals the causeway which crosses the dangerous rocks surrounding the island. Built in 1898 and some 120ft (36.5m) high, the lighthouse has a birdwatching hide and visitor centre open to the public. As well as a popular recreational destination it houses permanent and changing exhibitions and offers educational facilities for local people. It is thought that the monks from Tynemouth had a chapel on the north side of the island and also a tower with an additional storey where a lantern was kept burning.

From the light's platform the view of the coast slips away southwards towards Whitley Bay, Cullercoats and the mouth of the Tyne. Opposite the island, sometimes called Bate's or Bait Island, is Curry's Point, where the body of Michael Curry was hung in chains after he was executed for murder in 1739.

Cullercoats

The lifeboat station at Cullercoats must be one of the most colourfully decorated in the country. The lifeboat was established here in 1852 and the boat today is an inshore inflatable lifeboat that can reach 32 knots.

Cullercoats was originally a small fishing village and at one point had 15 cobles operating from the port; salt was also exported from here and it is recorded that the *Fortune of Whitby* sailed in July 1726 with 21 tons on board. Today the beach is very popular with Tynesiders and the Dove Marine Laboratory, an important facility for marine science, is sited here.

Cullercoats was particularly popular with artists in the later years of the 19th century and work by the "Cullercoats Group" is now sought after by collectors. The American artist Winslow Homer spent two years in the town in the late 19th century producing many famous watercolours.

Tynemouth Longsands

Tynemouth Longsands stretches northwards backed by the town and sand dunes. The beach is very popular for those wanting to bathe, surf or simply relax. Nearby is a park, sealife centre, toy museum and shops, making it an ideal seaside destination.

The cliffs at Tynemouth offer an excellent vantage point from which to watch ships entering the Tyne estuary, especially when magnificent sailing ships call at Newcastle in the annual Tall Ships Race.

In 1845 the pillar that supports the huge statue of Admiral Collingwood, Nelson's second-in-command at Trafalgar, was erected and just below are the cruel rocks called the Black Middens upon which many boats and lives have been lost. Local legend has it that the rocks were thrown there by the devil in an attempt to curb the wealthy sea trade of Newcastle. The Tynemouth Life Brigade was formed in December 1869 and was the first such volunteer association in the country. Today the village itself is a conservation area largely made up of buildings from the 18th and 19th centuries.

Tynemouth Priory

Perched on a clifftop, Tynemouth Priory is protected both by the sea and Tynemouth Castle, and is one of the largest fortified sites in the country. Originally the site was occupied by a 7th-century Saxon church, renowned as the burial place of St Oswin, king and martyr. The early monastery was sacked by the Danes in 800. The present buildings date from 1085 when a group of Benedictine monks from the abbey at St Albans arrived here; the monastery was finally completed at the end of the 13th century. The monks amassed great wealth from the coal industry which they used to finance the building work.

Tynemouth Castle

The massive gatehouse at Tynemouth Castle is an extension of the fortifications of the priory. The first castle here was a motte and bailey affair with a wooden palisade. The middle ages saw the castle act as a place of sanctuary. Charles I strengthened its defences and during the Civil War it was besieged and captured by both Royalist and Parliamentary forces. During the Second World War the castle was used as the base for a coastal defence unit.

South Shields

Marsden Rock is sited on a beautiful stretch of the north-east coast and is one of the most spectacular rock formations in Britain. Renowned for the thousands of pairs of seabirds that nest here, the rock was even more dramatic prior to 1996 when the arch that joined the present two stacks collapsed into the sea.

The rocks here are reputedly haunted by the ghost of John the Jibber. It is rumoured that he died a lingering death suspended in a bucket halfway down the cliff, having betrayed his fellow smugglers to the customs men.

As well as the beaches, the Marsden Grotto is popular. The origins of this pub date back to 1782, when an Allenheads leadminer nicknamed "Jack the Blaster" came to work in the limestone quarries at Marsden.

South Shields Customs House

South Shields Custom House was built in the 1860s at a time when the Tyne was a busy trading river. By the 1960s the Customs House was almost derelict but today it has become a successful arts and entertainment centre for the people of South Tyneside.

The South Shields Lifeboat Memorial is dedicated to the designers and crews of the early lifeboats; in 1829 the entire crew of 20 men were drowned when the town's lifeboat was lost. Willie Wouldhave, who lived in South Shields but who hailed from north of the river, designed the first self-righting lifeboat in 1789. The boat was lined with cork which made it almost impossible to capsize.

Arbeia Roman Fort and Museum

The reconstruction of the West Gate, the excavated remains and the finds discovered at the Roman fort of Arbeia are one of the success stories of modern tourism. Four miles to the east of the end of Hadrian's Wall at South Shields the fort guarded the entrance to the river Tyne from incursion by sea. It was constructed around AD160 and played a vital role in the running of the wall. Originally built to house a cavalry garrison, the fort's role changed around AD208 when it became the military supply depot for the 17 forts along the wall and other parts of the Roman frontier defensive system such as watchtowers and signalling stations. Among the treasures to be seen here are the remains of the granaries and one of the finest examples of a Roman commanding officer's house in Britain.

Segedunum

The 100ft high (30.5m) viewing tower at Segedunum, Wallsend offers amazing views of the most easterly Roman fort of Hadrian's Wall, sections of the wall and the river Tyne. The site also has a working reconstructed Roman bath-house, the only one of its kind in Britain. Segedunum is the largest Roman museum on Hadrian's Wall and features site finds together with the latest computer interactive displays. The wall originally finished at Newcastle before the Romans decided to extend it a further 3.5 miles (5.5km) eastwards to the new fort at Wallsend, housing a mixed unit of infantry soldiers and cavalry-troopers

On the south bank of the Tyne, the walls of Jarrow bear witness to some of the great events of early church history. The monastery of St Paul's at Jarrow was founded around 681. An earlier monastery, St Peter's, was founded close by at Wearmouth and the two centres were often referred to jointly as the monastery of Wearmouth Jarrow. Bede described them as "one monastery in two places". Bede was born in 673, and educated in the monastery from the age of seven. He is regarded as the founder of medieval historical writing and the first historian of the English people.

North Shields

The fish quay at North Shields with its distinctive lighthouse (left) is one of the best-known views in the north-east. Although much diminished from earlier days, fishing is still important here. Today the town remains an important commercial centre and the modern Royal Quays shopping centre attracts thousands to the town. North Shields has had its share of tragedy in wartime: in 1941 a single bomb from a lone German raider scored a direct hit on the air raid shelter of the Wilkinson Lemonade factory killing 105 people.

Further down the coast is the Souter Lighthouse (above). Opened in 1871, it was the first in the world to use electric current. To the north is the Leas: two and a half miles of cliffs, beaches and grassland with spectacular views. To the south Whitburn Coastal Park offers similar pleasures. The lighthouse was decommissioned in 1988 and now belongs to the National Trust. One of the cottages has been restored to provide a fascinating insight into the past lives of the lighthouse-keepers.

Tall ships

In the days of sail, boats would be moored three-deep along the quayside stretching all the way to Ouseburn. Those days are unlikely to return. But once every few years, Newcastle goes back in time to its maritime past when the Tall Ships visit the city. For a few days, the quayside once again has a mass of ships moored below the Tyne Bridge.

Since the 1980s a wave of regeneration has swept through Quayside. On Sunday mornings the area from the Tyne Bridge eastwards is a hive of activity as the Quayside Market takes place until mid afternoon. When the shopping fever has died down many visitors retire to the quayside pubs or restaurants for lunch and a chat. In the evening, the area is alive with laughter and noise as it must have been in the days of sail.

Tyne bridges

An autumn sunset bathes the Tyne and her bridges in an orange light. The Tyne bridges hold a special place in the history of the north-east; they have performed a vitally important role in the region's social and economic development throughout the ages. Each of the bridges has its own story to tell. The Swing Bridge opened in 1876 and was specially designed to allow large ships to pass upriver. The High Level Bridge, which opened in 1850, is one of the most important structures in the history of the British railway system. Robert Stephenson's bridge brought Newcastle into the London-Edinburgh railway link and confirmed the East Coast line as the major rail route between the two cities. Opened by King George V in 1928 the Tyne Bridge is used by approximately 60,000 vehicles a day and was originally intended to have massive triumphal arches at each end. It is now associated with the swarming mass of runners crossing it as part of the Great North Run.

Millennium Bridge at night

The lighting beneath the pedestrian deck of the Gateshead Millennium Bridge causes an almost mirror-like appearance on the surface of the slow moving river Tyne. The arch is lit with a series of high-powered lights which change colour, the display blending in seamlessly with the buildings of Newcastle and Gateshead on either bank. The bridge creates a circular promenade in conjunction with the Swing Bridge that allows people to enjoy and appreciate both of the newly revitalised banks of the river. This walk is especially popular at night when separate sections are illuminated in different colours.

Building the bridge

Europe's largest floating crane, the *Asian Hercules II*, transported the bridge six miles up the river to its present position in November 2000. In certain places the bridge was wider than the river and it had to be turned sideways to continue its journey.

When it was opened in 2001 the Millennium Bridge had cost over £22m. Amazingly the bridge can be raised and lowered, silently, in only four minutes. When open, it allows ships 82ft (25m) headroom, the same as the clearance of the Tyne Bridge. When closed the clearance is 15.5ft (4.7m) and the navigation channel is 98.5ft (30m) wide, equal to that of the neighbouring Armstrong Swing Bridge.

Art in Newcastle

The splendid Baltic Arts Centre (above) is a superb addition to the Newcastle-Gateshead scene. This magnificent warehouse was formerly a flour mill, where grain was stored before being loaded onto ships for export. The £46m arts centre opened in 2002 and has 3,000sq m of galleries, a cinema, lecture theatre, workshops and artists' studios. It is the largest venue for contemporary art outside London. The Millennium Bridge has provided a stylish link between the Newcastle and Gateshead Quays for pedestrians and visitors.

Art has become far more accessible to the public either side of the river, from outdoor attractions such as the Swirle Pavilion and the bronze Vulcan statue (left) by Sir Eduardo Paolozzi, to exhibitions by artists at the Baltic Arts Centre. Where industrial warehouses once stood, the Quayside now has office blocks and hotels bordering the river. The Copthorne Hotel (right) lies on the Newcastle bank close to the High Level Bridge and is just one of the many elegant new hotels that have sprung up along the river bank.

The Sage

The Sage Gateshead is a centre for music and the performing arts. The dramatic glass and stainless steel building on the south Quayside was designed by Sir Norman Foster and has been likened to a "resting armadillo". It has a 1,700 seat hall plus a flexible 450-seat auditorium and the interior of the building with its innovative walkways, stairs and brilliant lighting is a superb example of modern architecture.

Around the front and sides of the Sage is a glazed concourse that provides stunning views of the Quayside and river. The roof of this incredible building holds over 3,500sq m of glass; this allows light to flood the building during the day and provides a colourful spectacle when the building is viewed from outside after dark.

Civic Centre

Bathed in a blue light that seems to represent the waters of the Tyne, Newcastle's Civic Centre reflects much of the history and culture of this great city. Twelve seahorse heads cast in bronze, part of Newcastle's coat of arms, adorn the top of the tower. The heads are approximately 5ft (1.5m) in diameter. Sixteen feet (5m) up the exterior wall is a sandstone statue of the river god (below), with water pouring out of his outstretched hand.

This imposing building has three wings arranged round a courtyard and a 12-storey main block to the north, capped by a copper lantern and beacon and a circular debating chamber to the west. King Olaf of Norway officially opened the Civic Centre in 1968. The city's links with the countries of Scandinavia are symbolised by the bronze statue of swans soaring into flight in the courtyard.

Castle keep

The keep is all that remains today of the "new castle" that gave the city its name. It was constructed as part of the rebuilding in stone of the castle carried out by Henry II and took 10 years to complete. Even today, this imposing structure gives an impression of immense military power. Newcastle Corporation supplied cannons to the keep to be fired on ceremonial occasions. This ended in tragedy in 1812 when one of the cannons exploded and a gunner was blown over the parapet.

Next to the keep is the Black Gate, which dates back to before 1649. The slots which held the counterweights of the drawbridge are still clearly visible. Today, it is difficult to imagine that in the 19th century the Black Gate contained a pub and shops, and was home to more than one hundred people. By 1855 the building had become a tenement used as a centre for secondhand shoe and clothes dealers. The gate even contained a popular pub, The Two Bulls' Heads.

Grey Street

Built in 1836 by John Dobson and Richard Grainger, Grey Street has often been referred to as "England's finest street". Indeed the imposing Regency buildings that sit either side of this gently curving thoroughfare have now become recognised as a style of architecture known as "Tyneside Classical". The heritage-led Grainger Town partnership has recently restored much of Newcastle city centre to its former glory including Grey Street. The pavements have been upgraded too, using Caithness stone from Scotland, Newcastle's original paving material.

In recent years Newcastle has become one of the loveliest illuminated cities in the country. City centre streets have been enhanced at night by lighting, especially now that the beautiful stonework has been cleaned and its natural colours exposed. One example of this is the Theatre Royal; its distinctive portico has six massive Corinthian columns rising up from enormous moulded plinths supporting a classical triangular pediment bearing the Royal Coat of Arms. The original Theatre Royal was located on Mosley Street; keen to incorporate a theatre into his newly designed city centre, Richard Grainger paid hefty compensation to close the old theatre and re-locate it to Grey Street. The new theatre opened in February 1837.

Earl Grey's monument

The man from whom Grey Street gets its name, prime minister Earl Grey, is celebrated in a monument sited at the top of Grainger Street. The twice life-size statue was sculpted in 1838 by Edward Hodges Bailey, who was also responsible for Nelson's statue in Trafalgar Square. In the 19th century there were lights on top of the monument which were lit in the event of an accident occurring in the city: red lights indicated fatalities; white lights meant that all the participants had survived. The low platform at the base of the monument is a popular meeting place for shoppers.

Central Station

To many people the beauty of Central Station is the magnificent Victorian ironworked roofing with its majestic pillars and glass ceiling. The roof was unique at the time and won its designer, Charles Dobson, a prize at the Newcastle exhibition. The original six huge doors to the station, with their intricate iron latticework, still remain as does the first-class waiting room, which is now a popular bar and restaurant (right). Built between 1845 and 1850, the station and Neville Street, which was constructed at the same time, swept away a stretch of the 13th-century city wall. Just to the east of the booking hall stood the West Spital Tower. Countless citizens of Newcastle have walked under the portico to enter the station but this was a later addition built in 1863 to a design by Thomas Prosser. The station was opened by Queen Victoria in 1850; local legend has it that the monarch was not impressed when shown the bill!

City panorama

This view taken from the castle keep towards Newcastle's Moot Hall shows many of the major sights of both Newcastle and Gateshead through the ages, from the old city walls in the foreground to the Tyne Bridges and the new buildings of the Quayside in the distance. The city's 13th-century walls butt up against the Moot Hall now standing in the old courtyard of the castle, opposite the keep. William Stokoe designed the hall in 1810 in a Greek Doric and Pediment style. Further back, the 19th-century Swing Bridge is dominated by the 20th-century Tyne Bridge in the centre of the photograph. From the 21st century the "glass armadillo" of the Sage Gateshead on the far bank of the river and the curve of the Gateshead Millennium Bridge catch the eye.

St James' Park

The stadium (right), home of Newcastle FC, dominates the area just to the north of the city centre. The club, known as the Magpies – because of their distinctive black and white strip – have a loyal following in the city.

71

Jesmond Dene

A wooded valley which runs alongside the river Ouseburn between South Gosforth and Jesmond Vale, Jesmond Dene is rich in wildlife. Its exotic trees and shrubs, miles of footpaths and waterfalls provide a wonderful "green corridor" close to the heart of the city. It was formerly an industrialised valley that housed quarrying and ordnance testing. In 1835 William Armstrong, the famous north-east industrialist, acquired the land partly to build a banqueting house to entertain his clients and also to build Jesmond Dean as a family home. Armstrong's philanthropy transformed the area from an industrial valley. By the 1870s Armstrong was spending much of his time at his new home at Cragside; in 1883 he donated the valley and gardens to the townspeople of Newcastle. Unfortunately the banqueting house is now a ruin and Jesmond Dean is no longer in existence.

Saltwell Towers

Saltwell Park, based in the heart of Gateshead, is one of Britain's finest examples of a Victorian park. Opened to the public in 1876 when the park was bought for the people of the town by Gateshead Corporation, it is still known as "the people's park". Saltwell Park contains 11 listed buildings and monuments, including the magnificent Gothic mansion of Saltwell Towers and its gardens which were built between 1850 and 1862, one of two contrasting Victorian landscapes here. The other is the mid 19th-century parkland designed by Edward Kemp which consists of a series of gardens in different styles, from an open meadow to a formal Italianate garden.

Gibside

The Gibside Estate (left and right) was the property of the coal magnate George Bowes who developed this great "forest garden" over 200 years ago. It is now owned by the National Trust and

offers the visitor 15 miles of woodland and walks beside the river Derwent with dramatic romantic ruins. This wonderful 18th-century forest garden is only three miles from the Metro Centre and visitors can enjoy the Octagonal and Lily Ponds, the Orangery and the Banqueting House, now a Landmark Trust property.

Gibside Chapel was designed by James Paine and built as a mausoleum in the 1760s for George Bowes. Famous for its unusual three-tiered pulpit, it has today become a popular venue for weddings.

The chapel was consecrated in 1812 and the mausoleum beneath the chapel is a plain circular vaulted chamber with a central column from which burial niches radiate around the walls. An avenue extends from the chapel to an obelisk with a statue of British Liberty also designed by Paine in 1757.

The Hoppings

The huge fairground called the Hoppings is best seen at night when tens of thousands of coloured lightbulbs burn brightly across the Town Moor. The Newcastle Hoppings is Europe's largest travelling fair and each year attracts hordes of visitors to the Moor in the last week of June. Local folklore has it that the rain that often accompanies the fair is the result of a Romany curse.

The Temperance Fair held on the Town Moor was the forerunner of the Hoppings. There were children's games, sports and music and at the end of the day those gathered would feast and drink and then dance or "hop" around bonfires to the music of local pipers or fiddlers. These gatherings or fairs consequently became known as the "Hoppings".

Angel of the North

Constructed from sections transported to the site in 1998 and overlooking the A1, it is estimated that at least 90,000 motorists a day pass Antony Gormley's *Angel of the North*; it can also be seen clearly by rail passengers on the East Coast mainline from London to Edinburgh. Few realise the statue is actually hollow to allow for internal inspections with an access door on one of the shoulder blades, and that it is built on the site of a former colliery pit-head baths. It is taller than four double-decker buses and its wings are almost as long as those of a Jumbo jet. The Angel is made of weather resistant Cor-ten steel, containing a small amount of copper, which forms a patina on the surface that mellows with age and contains enough steel to make four Chieftain tanks. In its exposed, hillside position, the statue has been designed to withstand winds of 100mph.

Sunderland Bridge

Built in 1929 the Wearmouth Bridge crosses the river Wear linking
Sunderland with Hylton and Monkwearmouth on the north of the river.
When it was erected in 1796, the original bridge was the longest single-span
cast iron bridge in the world. The railway bridge behind was built in 1879
and extended the railway south from Monkwearmouth to the centre of
Sunderland. In the mid 17th century the proximity of the Durham coalfield
to the city necessitated new port facilities and an expansion in shipbuilding.
By 1840 there were 65 shipyards on the river and Sunderland took its place as
the biggest shipbuilding port in the world. The last coalmine, the
Monkwearmouth Colliery, closed in 1993 and today is the site of the Stadium
of Light, home to Sunderland FC. Sunderland was awarded city status in 1992.

   Like many industrial cities of the north-east, Sunderland has undergone a
renaissance in its town planning and quality of life. In addition to riverside
walks and public art it now boasts a new marina complex that includes
moorings, new housing and a watersports centre.

Hylton Castle

Hylton Castle is a medieval gatehouse and tower in Hylton Dene, Sunderland. The castle stood guard over an important ferry crossing of the Wear and is most famous for its ghost called the "Cauld Lad o' Hylton", a stable boy cruelly murdered by his master. The keep, four main walls and part of the chapel are all still standing. Over the years, the Castle and Dene had become neglected and vandalised. In 1992 a group of local residents set to work restoring the Dene and planning for its future. It is now in the care of English Heritage.

Sunderland Minster

Situated in the city centre, Sunderland Minster, St Michael's and All Angels, was originally a small medieval village church. The present church, however, is mainly 19th century with medieval fragments incorporated into the fabric. The building was inaugurated as the Minster for the City of Sunderland in January 1998.

Sunderland Winter Gardens

Sunderland's Winter Gardens house a superb botanical collection of over 1,500 plants of 146 species in naturalistic settings under a single-span 98.5ft (30m) dome. The gardens display samples of many important plants from around the world and visitors can take a staircase or scenic lift up to a treetop walkway where they can look down into an amazing rainforest canopy below. The gardens also house a number of exotic palms from countries such as Australia, Madagascar and Malaysia. The Winter Gardens are linked to Sunderland's remodelled museum and the upgraded and re-landscaped Mowbray Park in the city centre. Visitors enter the museum via a striking new glazed entrance which leads into the "museum street".

Sunderland Empire

The Sunderland Empire with its distinctive tower topped off with a turreted dome and silver globe is a well-loved landmark in the city. The Empire's internal layout is virtually unique in theatre design since the side "slipper seats" almost border the stage. The foundation stone of the theatre was laid on September 29 1906 and in July 1907 the Edwardian music hall favourite Vesta Tilley declared the Empire open when performing on stage.

The theatre was originally called the Empire Palace and on opening it had a 3,000-seat auditorium. Today the capacity has been reduced to around 1,900. Legendary comedy stars Stan Laurel and Charlie Chaplin performed here; tragically, on the opening night of *The Mating Season* in 1976, the actor Sid James of *Carry On* fame died on stage after suffering a heart attack.

In 2004 the Empire re-opened after a £4.5m refit with a production of Andrew Lloyd Webber's *Starlight Express*. The work carried out during a nine-month closure included the complete rebuilding of the stage, the construction of a new orchestra pit plus work to the roof and backstage areas. The Sunderland Empire is currently the only theatre between Manchester and Edinburgh capable of staging large-scale West End productions.

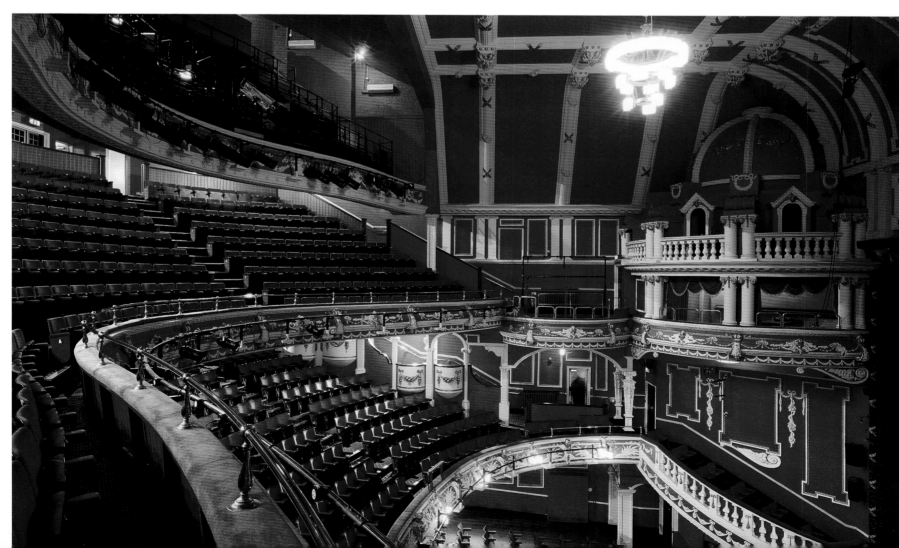

Fulwell Mill

A unique Sunderland landmark, Fulwell Mill is the only working windmill in north-east England. It was built in 1821 and has recently been restored. Visitors can enjoy demonstrations of the ancient art of cornmilling and get an insight into the life of the workings of a 19th-century windmill.

Penshaw Monument

Built in 1844 by private subscription and designed by John and Benjamin Green of Newcastle, the Penshaw Monument is unusual in that it has no inscription. Built in the form of a 100ft (30.5m) long, 50ft (15m) wide and 70ft (21m) high ruined Greek temple, the monument is based on the Thesion, the Temple of Theseus in Athens. It commemorates John George Lambton, first Earl of Durham (known as Radical Jack). Located opposite Herrington Country Park, its high position astride Penshaw Hill gives views as far afield as Durham Cathedral and the north Pennines. Local folklore has it that the legendary Lambton Worm, a fearsome dragon, wound itself 10 times around Penshaw Hill.

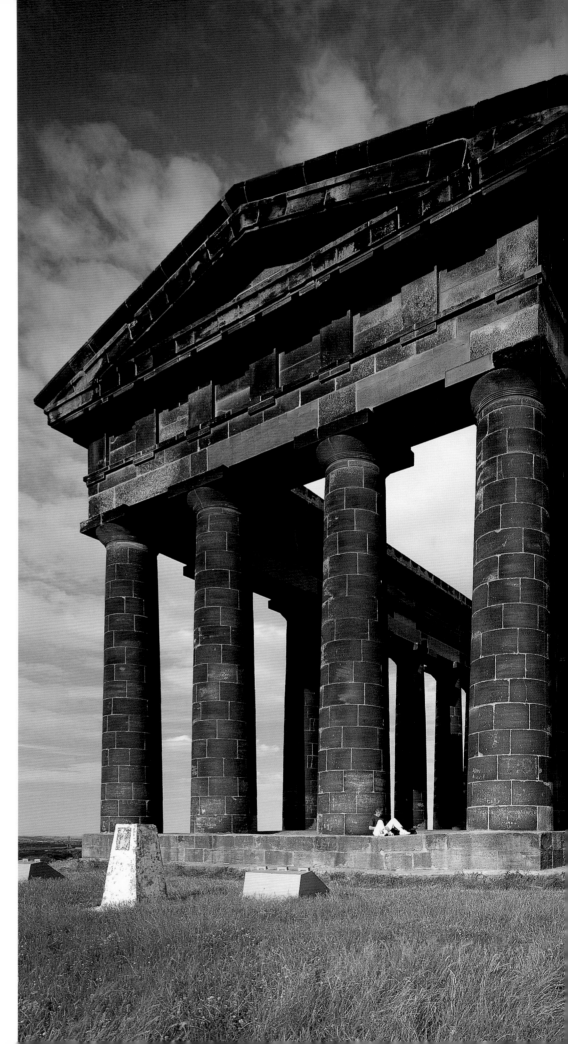

Glass Centre

Set on the north bank of the river Wear, the award-winning National Glass Centre is a stunning building and acts as a base for artists, designers and makers to meet and create new products and artworks. The University of Sunderland's Glass, Architectural Glass and Ceramics Departments are located in the centre as is the International Institute for Research in Glass.

University of Sunderland

Sunderland University has two main sites within the city. Perched on the north bank of the river Wear, the Sir Tom Cowie Campus at St Peter's houses the Sunderland Business School, the impressive David Goldman Informatics Centre and the Media Centre. St Peter's Campus has several modern buildings arranged around a large open plaza, called University Square.

County Durham

Durham is one of the most visually attractive cities in Britain. Modern and ancient buildings, including its world famous castle and cathedral (right and below), are jammed together on a narrow site created as the river Wear flows in a hairpin bend, almost encircling a huge outcrop of sandstone on which the town is built. It is little wonder that this collection of historic buildings has been designated as a World Heritage Site. But the county of Durham is more than the city which bears its name. It contains pretty fortified towns and castles including Raby, Brancepeth and Barnard Castle, outstanding museums such as those at Beamish and Bowes, ecclesiastical ruins like those at Egglestone Abbey and elegant towns such as Bishop Auckland. The roots of Christianity in Britain go deep in County Durham – monks from Holy Island sought shelter in the towns and cities of the area and helped establish them as important religious settlements. The remains of the Venerable Bede and St Cuthbert are interred at Durham Cathedral.

Durham Cathedral

Begun by Bishop William of Calais in 1093, Durham Cathedral is an outstanding example of Romanesque architecture. The cathedral is famous for the spiral and zig-zag decorated columns in the nave, whilst the arches that divide the nave into the separate sections are amongst the earliest pointed examples in Europe. The cathedral has been a centre for pilgrimage throughout its 900-year history. It contains the tombs of St Cuthbert, the saintly seventh-century bishop of Lindisfarne and that of the Venerable Bede, the first English historian, which were placed there in 1370.

There have been occasions over the centuries when the cathedral has suffered damage and vandalism. The 14th-century altar screen originally contained 107 alabaster figures but many were vandalised in the 16th century. In 1650 further damage was caused when Cromwell imprisoned 4,000 Scots there. One of the most beautiful features of the cathedral today is the huge rose window with its central core depicting Christ surrounded by the apostles; it was created in the 15th century and reconstructed in the 18th.

Cathedral cloisters

The cloisters adjoin the south side of the cathedral and are clustered around a small square green known as the Cloister Garth. The four covered cloister walkways were designed so that monks would have shelter when relaxing, studying and praying. The walkway on the northern side of the cloisters by the main cathedral wall was formerly the monk's scriptorium and it contained a number of reading chambers for study. The buildings surrounding the Cloister Garth were the monastic priory buildings and included the refectory, the chapter house, the monk's dormitory and the kitchen.

Durham Castle

Durham Castle is a fine example of the Norman motte and bailey style of fortification. Building began in 1072 with a circular keep on top of the hill overlooking the town as a part of William the Conqueror's plan to pacify the region; the castle was enlarged in 1174. During the middle ages, Durham was one of a number of castles spread throughout the north to counter the threat of invasion from the Scots. Later it was taken over as the principal residence of the Bishops of Durham or the Prince Bishops as they were known, since they administered the county on behalf of the Crown. It was they who built the magnificent halls and chapel, rare survivors of secular Norman splendour. The medieval bishops continued to develop the castle and in the 17th century yet more lavish accommodation was provided. In the 1830s the bishops left the castle and it became part of the University of Durham.

Durham Castle Gatehouse

To the west of the Gatehouse is the Great Hall probably built by Bishop Anthony Bek (1284-1311) in the 13th and 14th centuries and now used as the dining hall of the university – serving much the same purpose as was originally intended. The basement of the hall now houses wine cellars. Opposite the Gatehouse is one of the oldest parts of the castle, built by Bishop Pudsey (1153-1195). The keep is not original but is a Victorian replica built to the original plans.

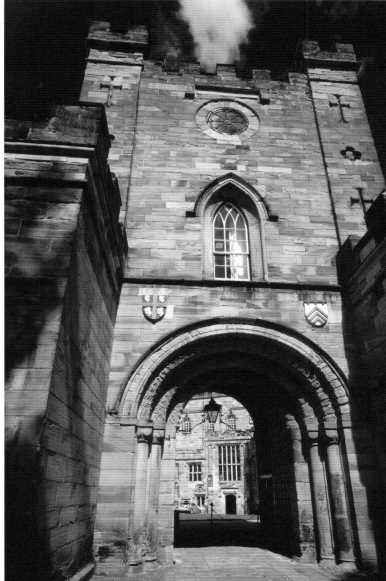

Durham Market Place

Durham's cobbled Market Place, site of the town hall and Guildhall, has medieval origins but the present Market Square is largely of Victorian origin. In the summer visitors can often enjoy street entertainment set amongst the stunning floral displays. Built in 1858, the spire of the Church of St Nicholas dominates the eastern side of the Market Place. The Victorian church of St Nicholas replaced a medieval church which dated from the early part of the 12th century. Unlike the present church this building had a tower rather than a spire. Today much of Durham's shopping area is closed to modern traffic, making for a relaxed atmosphere. The city is very compact yet still offers a wide range of facilities to the visitor and a variety of shops and restaurants co-exist happily with the Victorian market.

Crook Hall

The beautiful medieval manor house of Crook Hall has a banqueting hall and a 17th-century Jacobean room. The hall is thought to have been built in the 13th century but it may well be even older. The building is best known for its four beautiful gardens, one of which concentrates on plants which were grown in Shakespeare's time. Lying close to the centre of the town and the banks of the river Wear, it is one of a number of historic sites that are easily reached on foot via the many bridges and footpaths of the city.

Prebends Bridge

A stroll along the Durham Riverbanks is a must for any visitor to the city. The best view of Durham Cathedral, with its western towers soaring majestically above the wooded river bank, is from Prebends Bridge, which was built in 1777. The bridge formed a major part of the Durham Riverbanks Gardens which surrounded the peninsula from the 16th to the 18th centuries, and today it also offers fine views of the weir and Fulling Mill, now part of the university. There are three other ancient monuments within the Riverbanks area – Elvet Bridge, the Water Gate and Framwellgate Bridge.

89

Brancepeth Castle

Built in the 11th century, Brancepeth Castle has played a major role in the history of the region. Originally the home of a Saxon lord, it eventually became the property of the Nevilles until confiscated by Elizabeth I. Sir Henry Bellaysyse, who owned the castle in the early 18th century, had a daughter, Mary, who became attracted to a local man, Bobby Shaftoe. Her love for Bobby became the subject of the famous song. In 1796 William Russell, a broker from Sunderland, bought the castle; his son Matthew, who re-built the castle, owned numerous coalmines in the area and was alleged to be the richest commoner in England. The poet Tennyson was a regular visitor during the 19th century and the castle continued to be occupied until the First World War when it became a military hospital. It remained empty until the start of the Second World War when it became the headquarters of the Durham Light Infantry.

Brancepeth

Brancepeth is a quiet attractive village distinguished by the creeper-covered cottages leading up to the castle gates. Old-fashioned street lights line the streets and there is an ancient bench taken from the old railway station that once stood on the outskirts of the village. The first-recorded village rector was a monk from Durham called Haeming who has left a signature dating back to 1085. Alfred, Lord Tennyson, Poet Laureate from 1850 to 1892, wrote his famous poem *Maud* at Brancepeth.

Beamish open air museum

The world-famous open air museum at Beamish was set up in 1970 and tells the story of the people of the north-east of England at two important points of their history – in 1825 and 1913. The museum is made up of old buildings from the region. Some, such as the Drift Mine, Home Farm and Pockerley Manor were already on the site; others have been brought from their original location and carefully reconstructed. There are no labels or glass cases at Beamish; the idea is to give visitors a realistic view of life in the past. Staff are dressed in costume and the feeling is much more of being part of a theatrical production than walking the aisles of a traditional museum.

Beamish attractions

Around 350,000 people visit the museum annually. Beamish is a past winner of both the British and European Museum of the Year awards. Clydesdale heavy horses were once a common site in the north of England and at Beamish they can be seen in the horseyard and working around the museum. Visitors can choose between a reconstructed high street (left) or a Victorian park and railway station. The museum also has a Victorian fairground which includes a helter skelter and carousel.

Bishop's Palace

Auckland Castle has been the home of the Bishops of Durham – the "Bishop's Palace" – for over 800 years. Originally, this was a banqueting hall and hunting lodge built in the 12th century and was gradually developed for the Prince Bishops into one of the most ornate palaces in Britain. The magnificent chapel is believed to be the largest private place of worship in Europe. Although the Prince Bishops had a number of other residences, the castle seems to have been their favourite and in 1832 it became their official home.

Escomb Church (right)

This beautiful Saxon church to the west of Bishop Auckland dates from the 7th century and is one of northern Europe's finest examples of early Christian architecture. The church is constructed from stone from the nearby Binchester Roman fort and some of the stones still bear Latin inscriptions from the period. Unusually the church is not dedicated to any saint and is known simply as Escomb Church. Above the porch to the right is a sundial; this is part of the original construction and is probably the oldest sundial in the United Kingdom.

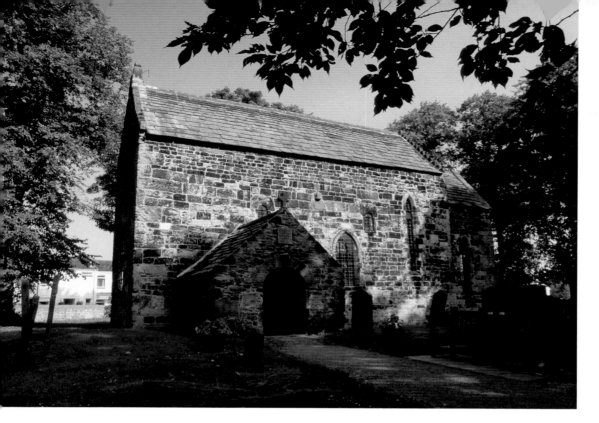

Bishop Auckland

Bishop Auckland is situated at the confluence of the river Wear and the river Gaunless and has been the site of an important market since medieval times. As the name implies, the town has been the seat of the Bishops of Durham since the 12th century. Bishop Auckland grew up around the gates of Auckland Castle which is still the official residence of the Bishops of Durham. Originally a Norman manor house and hunting lodge, today the castle stands in its own park east of the town's marketplace. The French-style town hall situated in the marketplace is a Grade I listed building. The main street in Bishop Auckland follows the course of the Roman Dere Street which led to the Roman fort of Binchester, just to the north of the town.

Raby Castle

Raby Castle is one of the largest and most impressive of England's medieval castles and is famous for its beautiful walled gardens and deer park. King Canute owned the estate in the early 11th century and may well have built the first castle here. The present building was begun by John, 3rd Baron Nevill in about 1360. The castle is in an excellent state of preservation and includes a sturdy gatehouse, complete with portcullis and "murder holes" for pouring oil on attackers. At the south-east corner of the castle is the Bulmer's Tower, almost unique in castle architecture

since it has five sides. The castle has a cavernous kitchen built in 1360 and a garrison room with walls between 10 and 20 feet thick. In 1569, 700 knights gathered in the medieval baron's hall to plot the doomed "Rising of the North" in support of Mary, Queen of Scots against Elizabeth I. In the 1840s the sumptuously furnished Octagon drawing room was added.

Staindrop

One of County Durham's most fascinating villages, Staindrop, just south of Raby Castle, is mostly made up of 18th-century stone houses surrounding a series of interlocking greens which are lined with limes and horse chestnuts. The main street is an attractive mix of stone cottages, some brightly painted, with the square steeple of St Mary's church dominating the view. The side roads still have signs of the many old workshops and stables that demonstrate the wealth of the village in the 18th and 19th centuries. In 1971 the centre of the village was designated a conservation area in order to protect its unique built environment.

Bowes Museum

This famous museum in Barnard Castle originated in a private foundation created between 1862 and 1875 by John and Josephine Bowes. It was conceived and purpose-built as a public art gallery by the French architect Jules Pellechet and opened in 1892. The building is designed in the style of a French chateau and has public galleries on three floors and a collection of European fine and decorative arts from the middle ages to early Victorian times. There is particular emphasis on the arts of France including items from the Bowes' home in Paris.

Perhaps the best known exhibit in the museum is the famous Silver Swan, a life-size musical automaton comprising a clockwork mechanism covered in silver plumage above a music box. In the 40 seconds of musical movement the swan turns its head to the left and right and appears to preen its back. It then spots a fish, bends down, catches and swallows its prey. As the music stops the swan resumes its upright position.

The collections

The Bowes Museum, housed in a typically French grand chateau, puts the visitor in mind of grand houses in the French countryside. It has some of the best collections of European art in Britain. French, Spanish and Italian paintings are a feature of the collection together with European ceramics and textiles. The museum also houses collections of archaeological finds from County Durham and artefacts showing the social history of Teesside. Bowes also contains a fine collection of posters by Toulouse Lautrec.

Rookhope

Rookhope lies snugly in the upper reaches of the Rookhope Burn and it is here that the earliest medieval references to mineral mining in this area are recorded. In 1153 King Stephen granted a licence for an iron mine and a lead mine in "Rychup". By the late 18th century the whole area was covered with smelting mills and littered with the distinctive giant chimneys and brick flues that helped carry the poisonous gases away from the workplaces. Outside the village on the road to Allenheads is "Rookhope Arch", the one remaining arch of a bridge that carried a two-mile long twin flue linked to the nearby smelt-mill. The roads to the village are very narrow but there are superb views across the north Pennines. On December 8th 1569, the valley was the setting for a border battle in which a large group of mosstroopers (cattle raiders) were caught after they had stolen a herd of cattle from Weardale. The event is remembered in the local ballad *The Rookhope Ryde.*

Stanhope Hall

The little market town of Stanhope, with its cobbled marketplace, lies 20 miles (30km) west of the city of Durham. In the middle ages, the Prince Bishops would hold "forest courts" in the town for locals accused of poaching. Just outside the village is Stanhope Hall, an attractive building which was the ancestral home of the Fetherstonhalgh family until the last male of the family was killed in the Civil War. William de Monte lived here in the middle of the 12th century in the reign of King Stephen.

Killhope

The Killhope lead-mining museum in Upper Weardale is a reconstructed mine powered by a water wheel, typical of the many leadmines operating in the north Pennines during the 19th century. The museum allows visitors to go underground and explore the working lives of the miners. The Park Level mine at Killhope was opened

in 1853 and for a few short years in the 1870s the mine was one of the richest in the whole of Britain. It ceased working around 1911 but reopened for a short while during the First World War.

Park Level Mill with its giant waterwheel was built in the late 1870s to help separate out the lead ore from waste. Today it is the only wheel that survives in the area.

Barnard Castle

Perched high atop a steep bank overlooking the river Tees, Barnard Castle was first built around the year 1095 and later fortifed again by Bernard Balliol in 1135. The castle gave its name to the town that grew up alongside it. Amongst later owners were the Prince Bishops and Richard III. The castle played an important part in the defeat of the northern Earls who rose against Elizabeth in 1569. The site was badly damaged in 1630 when Sir Henry Vane bought the building so that its stone

could be used to rebuild his home at Raby Castle. The town itself has a unique character and is recognised nationally as one of the most architecturally important towns in the United Kingdom. The Market Cross and the 12th-century

Church of St Mary are both fine features. The town is full of fascinating old shops and a wonderful centre for antique collectors. Charles Dickens stayed at The King's Head when researching his novel *Nicholas Nickleby*.

Egglestone Abbey

The ruins of Egglestone Abbey perch above a steep slope overlooking the river Tees just south of Barnard Castle. The abbey lies in the grounds of Egglestone Hall which has old walled gardens, winding paths and lawns as well as many rare plants and shrubs. It was founded in 1195 but was not wealthy compared to many other monastic houses and at times had problems maintaining the required number of brethren to retain its status as an abbey. The abbey also had to contend with regular raids by the Scots. After the Dissolution, the land was granted to Robert Streely in 1548. Like many Tudor landowners, he turned it into a prestigious house and this influence is still visible in the ruins today. In the 19th century much of the abbey was pulled down and some of the stonework was re-used to pave the stable yard at nearby Rokeby Hall.

Lumley Castle

Lumley Castle is a magnificent building set within nine acres of parkland, overlooking the river Wear and situated near Chester-le-Street. It was built in 1392 as a manor house and was later converted by Sir Ralph Lumley to the castle that can be seen today. Sir Ralph built four great corner towers and the intervening buildings as well as the main gateway on the east. Local legend has it that Lumley is haunted by Lily Lumley, a 14th-century lady of the manor and wife of Sir Ralph, who was apparently thrown down a well by two priests after she refused to convert to Catholicism when her husband was absent as Governor of Berwick.

In the 18th century the basement of the south-west tower was altered by Sir John Vanbrugh, the architect of Blenheim Palace and Seaton Delaval Hall in Northumberland. Today the castle is a hotel. It is often used by visiting international cricket teams, some of whom have checked out early because of the supposed ghostly goings on!

St Mary's, Chester-le-Street

The Parish Church of Saint Mary and Saint Cuthbert is one of the oldest churches in the north of England, and it contains a facsimile of the Lindisfarne Gospels, presented in 2005. The town's place in history is assured – the Romans had a fort here in AD122 which they called Congangium, and it was in the town that the Bible was first translated into English.

There has been a Christian community at Chester-le-Street since 883. In this year, monks from the abbey of Lindisfarne were fleeing Viking raids and carrying the body of Saint Cuthbert. Sheltering at Chester-le-Street they built a shrine which became, for more than a century, the Cathedral of the Kingdom of Northumbria. In 999 the monks took the coffin to Durham where it still lies today in Durham Cathedral.

Today the town has a thriving outdoor market which is held weekly on Tuesday, Friday and Saturday as well as boasting one of the most attractive county cricket grounds in the country.

Lanchester

Set in the beautiful valley of the river Browney, Lanchester's name is derived from that of the Roman fort of Longovicium situated half a mile to the south-west of the village itself. Built around AD140, the fort was home to about 1,000 soldiers from Spain and Germany. The village has a beautiful wide green lined with fascinating old stone houses and to the south-east is Burnhopeside Hall, the home of William Hedley, the inventor of the locomotive "Puffing Billy". The Norman church of All Saints has aisles that were built at the end of the 12th century and the arcades separating them from the nave on the north side have pillars that are monoliths and were probably brought from Longovicium. The church also has a large Roman altar that was discovered locally in 1893.

Buried in the churchyard is Canon William Greenwell, a keen angler who invented *The Greenwell Glory*, a popular fishing fly still used to day.

Hamsterley

Sunlight filters through the canopy of Hamsterley Forest, a stunningly beautiful mixed forest of deciduous and coniferous species lying between Teesdale and Weardale that covers some 4,942 acres (2,000ha). The forest holds what is reputed to be England's highest beech wood at 1,148ft (350m); lower down the valley there is a flower meadow which has been designated as a Site of Special Scientific Interest and is particularly noted for its fungi.

Causey Arch

Spanning almost 90ft (27m) of the Causey Burn gorge and towering 80ft (24m) above it, Causey Arch was designed by Ralph Wood and built between 1725-6; it is recognised as the oldest surviving single arch railway bridge in the world.

Wood is reputed to have used Roman technology to construct the bridge, making use of the steep sides of the valley to hold up the arch. The bridge was constructed to provide a link for coal transportation between Tanfield and the river Tyne. Now one of the principal attractions in the Beamish Country Park, it was restored and waterproofed by Durham County Council in 1981.

Nearby is the Tanfield Railway, which is claimed to be the world's oldest operating railway; opened in 1725 it ran commercially until 1962 and is now run by volunteers. Originally, horses hauled small wagons along wooden tracks but these were replaced in the 19th century by metal rails and locomotives.

Consett

Like some giant dismembered dinosaur's foot, the base of one of the steel sculptures of *Terris Novalis* almost dares the passer-by to come closer. The sculptures are found on the section of the Coast-to-Coast cycle route from Consett to Chester-le-Street and won their sculptor Tony Cragg the Turner Prize in 1988. Symbolising the economic regeneration of the Consett area the stainless-steel sculptures of 19th-century surveying instruments are 20ft (6m) high and 20 times the size of the originals. The sculptures overlook the site of the old Consett Steelworks which were once so closely linked to the town. The original ironworks were set up in 1840 on what was a bleak moorland hillside and as they grew the town of Consett developed beside them. In 1980 the Consett Steelworks closed causing a devastating blow to the town and community.

Today Consett has become a centre for business and retail serving the surrounding countryside and is the administrative centre for Derwentside council.

Tees Valley

The river Tees rises in the foothills of the north Pennines and flows east to meet the sea at Teesmouth (below), south of Hartlepool. The Upper Tees valley is characterised by its heather-clad moorland and rolling farmland interspersed with the scattered ruins of the area's industrial past – in particular leadmining. This upland area is rich in nationally renowned beauty spots which include the dramatic waterfalls at High Force and Cauldron Snout (left). It then flows past historic towns and villages which include Middleton-in-Teesdale and Darlington; in its final stretches it passes through towns and cities such as Stockton-on-Tees, Middlesbrough and Hartlepool which form the industrial heartland of the region. Although Teesside has a reputation as an area dominated by heavy industry and manufacturing, its beautiful countryside and regenerated urban areas make for an attractive and dynamic environment.

Holwick Scar

Four miles to the north-west of Middleton-in-Teesdale lies the magnificent escarpment of volcanic rock known as Holwick Scar. Part of the Great Whin Sill, the Scar faces north-east across upper Teesdale near the village of Holwick. This massive structure is often thought to look like an ancient stone castle as the nature of the crags is reminiscent of circular stone towers. The Scar forms part of a group of crags in Upper Teesdale, the others being Falcon Clints, Cronkley Scar, Raven Scar and Dineholm Scar. These crags are famous both for rare breeding birds such as peregrine falcon, raven and ring ouzel and their equally rare and fragile plant life – indeed some of the plant communities are specially protected under British and international legislation. They include trees, lichen and ferns; one of these plants is a microspecies of hawkweed only known in Upper Teesdale and not found anywhere else in the world.

Middleton-in-Teesdale

The Tees flows gently through the upper reaches of Teesdale some two miles north of High Force. At this point the river flows through villages that are rich in history. The largest of these is Middleton-in-Teesdale where in the 1880s the London Lead Company established its northern headquarters. The impact of this can still be seen in the many buildings that symbolise Victorian prosperity. The village is known to have existed since the time of the Norsemen when King Canute owned the land.

High Force

Not only is the waterfall of High Force an incredible visual spectacle it is also memorable for its sound, where the mumbling of the rapids turns into the dramatic ceaseless roaring boom of the water hitting the plunge pool beneath. Here the river Tees plunges 70ft (21m), making it the highest unbroken waterfall in the country. The water is brown, peaty and very cold, and forms impressive whirlpools and gives dramatic views. Beneath the falls is one of the largest remaining juniper woods in the country.

In addition to High Force there are two other waterfalls on this stretch of the Tees. Low Force is found about three miles away, whilst to the west approximately four miles away is Cauldron Snout, the highest waterfall in England. The cascade drops 200ft (61m) down a 450ft (137m) long series of rock steps. The name "force" comes from a Norse word meaning a waterfall.

Seaham Monument

The bronze and stainless-steel Seaham Monument is the start of the Seaham Cliff Timeline walk. The panels depict different periods and influences on the development of Seaham through the ages. Situated above the cliffs just north of the town and opposite Seaham Hall, the monument also provides a space for people to walk and exercise.

The Timeline walk has six sites along its clifftop route. One of these is the Vane Tempest car park where a sculpture in the form of a disc with two interpretive panels describes the ideas and plans the Londonderry family and the architect John Dobson had for the town of Seaham.

There are also pavement plaques that help tell the story. The green around the war memorial has been completely relaid and the area in the vicinity of the cenotaph has been improved with new paving stones and replanted flower beds.

Seaham Harbour

Northumbrian cobles bob gently in the shelter of Seaham harbour with their lobster pots stacked neatly on the quayside. Seaham town and harbour developed as a result of the coal industry, and the harbour was built by the Londonderry family in 1828. The collection of sea coal which was gathered from the beaches and sold in nearby Sunderland was an important activity which continued as late as the 1930s. Seaham also had a brick warehouse known as the Banana Yard for ripening bananas from the West Indies. Inside was a series of brick "warmers" shaped like tunnels to ripen the fruit. Today this busy port trades with Europe and specialises in handling bulk cargoes such as steel, logs and chemicals.

The Seaham Estate was purchased by the Milbanke family in 1678 and they built Seaham Hall in the reign of George III. Lord Byron married Annabella Milbanke in the drawing room of the house in 1815.

Horden

This view taken from the Durham coastal footpath looks over the site of the former Horden Colliery, opened in 1900 and once the largest in the world. The colliery was built close to the coast because most of the mineworkings were under the sea. In the 1950s, the colliery was producing 4,200 tonnes of coal per day and employed 6,000 workers. The mine finally closed in 1987. The coast around Horden was badly scarred by the dumping of colliery waste. Today the site has been cleaned up allowing the coastal grasslands to re-establish themselves.

Darlington

The clock that towers over Darlington is part of the former Town Hall building. Darlington is well-known for its parks and leafy suburbs and despite its long history, dating from Saxon times, the town centre mostly consists of Victorian and 20th-century buildings. A sublime exception is the 12th-century Church of

St Cuthbert, which stands on the banks of the river Skerne; it was built by Hugh Pudsey, one of the Prince Bishops of Durham, and is sometimes referred to as the "Lady of the North".

Darlington owes much of its growth to the great Quaker families who lived here in the 18th and 19th centuries. It is famed worldwide as the birthplace of the railways. The world's first public railway opened here on September 27 1825; as well as carrying coal to Stockton, the train had room for 600 passengers. Today Darlington's railway history is celebrated by a brick sculpture. Created in 1997 by David Mach, the sculpture contains 185,000 bricks and weighs 15,000 tonnes. It is modelled on the *Mallard*, the 1938 steam locomotive that reached a speed of 126mph, and was the long-time holder of the world rail speed record.

Stockton-on-Tees

The lights of Stockton's Teesquay Millennium Footbridge reflect on the waters of the river as the sun sets slowly behind. Stockton can trace its origins back to Saxon times whilst its market is first recorded as being held in 1310.

The town is well known for its railway connections; it also made another tremendous impact on the history of the world when in 1826 John Walker invented the friction match. The great comic and music hall entertainer Will Hay was born in Stockton and the famous Conservative politician and prime minister, Harold Macmillan, the Earl of Stockton, represented the town as its MP for many years.

The Tees Barrage has created a stretch of clean, high-quality deep water making the river Tees suitable for watersports including sailing, rowing, wind-surfing, water-skiing, kayaking and canoeing. A man-made white-water course can also be found on the Tees. A footbridge and cycleway has been built which allows the public to view the structure of the barrage from close quarters and also enjoy riverside walks and cycling along its banks.

Middlesbrough

The setting sun casts an eerie glow over the river Tees and Middlesbrough's famous Transporter Bridge. The bridge dominates the skyline and, with a clearance of 160ft (48m), was originally designed to allow tall ships to pass beneath. Opened on October 17 1911 by Prince Arthur of Connaught, this unique bridge with its central cradle that ferries cars and pedestrians across the river has become Middlesbrough's icon. Its gondola can carry 200 people or six cars and one minibus across the river in just two and a half minutes.

Today Middlesbrough Town Hall (right) is one of the most respected musical venues in the country hosting everything from international orchestras to world famous rock bands. Like the other cities of the north-east, Middlesbrough has invested in public art as part of its rejuvenation – containing fibre optics and mirrors, the 33ft (10m) high interactive stainless-steel obelisk at Binns Corner is a good example.

Newport Bridge

Light trails mark the route of the traffic as it streams across Newport Bridge – the first vertical lift bridge in Britain built so that the central section can be raised to allow ships to pass beneath. Opened by the Duke of York in 1934 it has a lifting span of 270ft (82m), is 66ft (20m) long and was built from 8,000 tons of Teesside steel and 28,000 tons of concrete; its towers are 182ft (55.5m) high. The lifting mechanism allows the road to be raised 100ft (30.5m) in one and a half minutes.

In 1801 Middlesbrough was no more than a small farmstead occupied by about a dozen people. The farm and surrounding land was bought by a group of Quaker businessmen from Darlington who set about building a port to export coal and other commodities; from these beginnings, the town of Middlesbrough was born.

The mid 19th century saw Middlesbrough's population grow exponentially – from 40 people in 1829 to 7,600 by 1851. In this year the discovery of iron ore in the Cleveland Hills prompted local businessmen to build Teesside's first blast furnace in the town. A mere nine years later the population had increased to 20,000.

The steel effect

The development of steel in Middlesbrough powered the local economy and soon the city was famous as the steel manufacturing centre of Teesside. Middlesbrough rapidly became renowned worldwide for the construction of bridges, thanks to the engineering skills of its local workforce. The most famous bridge ever built on Teesside was the Sydney Harbour Bridge of 1932, partly modelled on the 1929 Tyne Bridge. Left and above: the Transporter Bridge; right: the single-span Newport Lifting Bridge.

Hartlepool

The magnificent abbey Church of St Hilda dominates the approach by sea and land to the Hartlepool headland and nearby the old town walls of Hartlepool, completed in 1333, can still be seen. Mainly Early English, dating from 1185, St Hilda's is on the site of an abbey which flourished as early as 658.

Until the second quarter of the 19th century, Hartlepool was a collection of small, isolated villages, sand dunes and marshes. By the end of the century, however, it had become the fifth largest shipping port in the United Kingdom.

Hartlepool was a target for enemy firepower during the First World War. On the morning of December 16 1914 the German navy bombarded the town for 35 minutes, resulting in the deaths of 117 townsfolk.

Hartlepool Marina

The sun sets over Hartlepool Marina, one of the major signs of the successful regeneration of the town. The new marina has become an attractive focal point with waterside restaurants and promenades.

The marina is not restricted to pleasure craft and many working boats of differing sizes can be seen scattered around the piers. In the centre of the marina is the award-winning Historic Quay, a reproduction of an 18th-century seaport portraying sights, sounds and smells of sealife at the time. Dominating the marina area are the triple masts of *HMS Trincomalee*. Built of teak in India in 1817 she is the oldest fighting ship still afloat in the country. This beautiful sailing ship was first moored in West Hartlepool in 1862 and was used as a training ship for young recruits to the navy. In 1897 the *Trincomalee* was sold for scrap but she was rescued, repaired and once again became a training vessel in 1903. She saw service during the Second World War and continued in her training role until 1986.

Saltburn

The beach at Saltburn is a popular venue for surfing and is famous for its attractive walks. Tides can be treacherous here and care needs to be taken when walking beneath the 365ft (111m) high Huntcliff. Saltburn was once a fashionable resort for the Victorians with its own rail link and formal gardens. A miniature railway which still exists was constructed at around the same time.

Just behind the seafront an Italianate garden and an ancient wooded area called Rifts Wood make up the Saltburn Valley gardens; they merge with a nature reserve and offer the visitor a superb display of both ornamental plants and wildflowers. The town and beach were once a hotbed of smuggling and many reminders of this activity can still be seen in Saltburn.

Saltburn Pier

Saltburn Pier is the only remaining pier on the north-east coast and is now practically half its original length due to the pounding of the sea over the years. Completed in 1869 the pier was originally 1,400ft (427m) long; after restoration it was reopened in 1978 at its present length of 681ft (208m). It was however still in need of repair and further restoration work was completed in 2001.

Cliff lift

Saltburn Pier can be reached from the town by the cliff lift which was opened in 1884. This replaced the original vertical lift of 1870; it has two cars and visitors enter via a small booth at the top. The lift is the oldest water-balanced lift in the country and the cabins have been refurbished with stained-glass windows.

The pier is popular for fishing and gives stunning views of spectacular Huntcliff. To the south of the pier the beach is suddenly curtailed by the cliffs which rise up to Wansett Hill.

Staithes

The isolated and picturesque fishing village of Staithes developed on the end of a narrow headland, so most of the old town is clustered around the base of the cliffs, close to the water's edge. The alleys and little cottages of the village have remained much as they were in their 19th century heyday, when over 200 boats fished out of Staithes. In the summer the village becomes a honeypot for tourists.

As a young man, in 1745, Captain Cook was apprenticed in Staithes; visitors can discover more about his history by visiting the Captain

Cook and Staithes Heritage Centre, a converted chapel in the town.

In the late 19th century, when the railway opened up the east coast, Staithes became a magnet for more adventurous Victorian tourists. In a similar way to Cullercoats in Northumberland the village attracted a large number of number of artists who became known as the Staithes Group. Well-known members of the group include Dame Laura Knight and Joseph Bagshawe and their work can be found in major collections including Tate Britain in London.

Boulby

The sun rises over the sea transforming the waves at Boulby into a palette of oranges and yellows. The massive cliffs are the highest on the east coast of England and tower 665ft (203m) over the sands just to the north of Staithes. The village is thought to have come into existence because of the mining of alum in the middle ages. Today, 3,609ft (1100m) deep below the surface, physicists are working in the Boulby Mine, conducting experiments in their search for dark matter.

Boulby also has a sound mirror some 20 feet high. Now a Grade II listed building, it was probably built around 1916 to give early warning of enemy ships and aircraft during the First World War; later, the development of radar made sound mirrors obsolete.

Roseberry Topping

Roseberry Topping is one of the most distinctively-shaped hills in the country. Often referred to by locals as the "Matterhorn of Cleveland", its high summit is a popular tourist attraction as it provides excellent 360 degree views of the region. On a clear day it is possible to see as far as Teesside in one direction and the Yorkshire Dales in another.

Also known as Odin's Hill, "Topping", from "Toppen", is one of a number of old Norse words for a hill. Roseberry Topping is shaped rather like the breaking crest of a wave, thanks to a mining accident. In 1880 iron ore began to be mined by a local company to supply the foundries of nearby Middlesbrough. Mining stopped in 1920 but the following year a huge landslide occurred that created the hill's distinctive shape; it is thought that the collapse of the mineworkings caused this. Now in the care of the National Trust, a spur of the Cleveland Way footpath runs up to the summit.

Gisborough Priory

Gisborough Priory was founded by Robert de Brus in 1119, and was home to Augustinian monks. Robert was an ancestor of Robert the Bruce, whose father is buried here. The large church was destroyed by Henry VIII during the reformation but the huge east gable wall still stands and is an outstanding example of Gothic architecture showing the wealth of the priory. It was built immediately after a disastrous fire of 1289 and survived because it was used as a folly by some of the later owners. The 12th-century gatehouse still exists; it was the original entrance and is the oldest part of the priory still standing. Like other religious houses in the north the priory suffered from periodic raids by the Scots.

Roseberry Topping in the snow – in these wintry conditions the splendid nickname of the "Cleveland Matterhorn" is fully justified.